Time Capsule 2030

Also by Monique McVeigh:
Everyday Life Dimension Matrix™ (Spring 2021)

Monique McVeigh

Time Capsule 2030

Your 2030 Life and Goals

 **Blue Sand Publications**

Copyright © 2020 by Monique McVeigh

All rights reserved. No part of this book may be reproduced by any mechanical, photographic, or electronic process, or in the form of a phonographic recording; nor may it be stored in a retrieval system, transmitted, or otherwise be copied for public or private use – other than for "fair use" as brief quotations embodied in articles and reviews – without prior written permission of the publisher.

ISBN: 978-1-952004-01-8 (Hardcover)
ISBN: 978-1-952004-00-1 (Paperback)
ISBN: 978-1-952004-02-5 (E-book)

1st edition, January 2020

Cover design and interior design by Blue Muse

Editing and cover photo by Steven Gaskin

To my parents, for making difficult and selfless decisions in order to ensure my brother and I had access to the best education possible.

Acknowledgments

I extend my appreciation to Steven Gaskin and William Long for editing this book and helping me give shape to my ideas.

Contents of Contents

The Idea Was Born — *xiii*

Setting the Tone — *1*
    Time Capsule — 3
    For you — 5
    Today — 7
    Visualize — 9
    Happiness — 12
    Inventory — 14

Going Deeper — *17*
    Business/Career — 20
    Charity/Gratitude — 22
    Family/Friends/Romance — 24
    Financial — 26
    Fun/Recreation/Social — 28
    Health/Well-being — 30
    Personal Development — 32
    Spiritual — 34

Life Dimensions MatrixTM — *38*
    Time and Energy — 40
    Action Plan — 44
    Revisiting, Reviewing, and Updating — 45
    About Monique McVeigh — 46

Templates — *47*

"Far away in the sunshine are my highest inspirations. I may not reach them, but I can look up and see the beauty, believe in them, and try to follow where they lead."

Louisa May Alcott

Monique McVeigh

The Idea Was Born

The idea of this book was born in early 2019 while I was waiting to have surgery. During the seven weeks from the day of my first consultation with the surgeon to the day of the procedure, I did a lot of thinking.

Somehow, my brain seemed to be working overtime to retrieve random memories: my first job, classmates long forgotten, festivities I'd attended, and the sporting matches of my college years. Memories I had not recalled for years were popping up in my mind. I did not plan to recount my life, at least not consciously, but it was happening.

One day, I was having breakfast in a diner and suddenly remembered the Disney movie, The Kid. There's a scene where two of the characters discuss what would happen if you could have a conversation with your younger self. When I first saw the movie, I didn't think too much about this concept. I truly enjoyed the movie - it's very entertaining - but I was watching for pure entertainment value, not a life changing lesson.

As I waited for my omelet, I began to think, "maybe it would be nice to go back in time and tell my younger self what to do or not to do. Who to avoid, or who to seek out. Maybe give my younger self a list with situations to stay away from, or at least to be careful with, or moments to enjoy to the max because they were going to be unique. Perhaps I could save myself some anguish, time, tears and...

Then I stopped. I realized I would have avoided important moments; learning moments that, while not pleasant, had been a critical part of my development and preparation for the future.

If everything is perfect in our lives, we do not learn to appreciate our surroundings, relationships, and all the other details. We would take everything for granted.

The day of my surgery finally arrived, and I spent the following weeks focused on healing. I had a lot of time to think, and that's when the idea for this book was finalized.

Throughout my personal and professional life, I have always set goals. I do not remember when I started; it may have been early in elementary school, maybe even in kindergarten. During my twenty-year career as a finance executive collaborating with highly technical teams in companies ranked in the Fortune Top 100, there were always plans and goals for financial performance, project implementation, and reporting.

While recovering from the surgery, I thought, why not write a book that can help others to facilitate long-term personal planning? And since we are at the beginning of a new decade, why not focus on making long-term plans?

After all, there is no time machine to go to the past or future. We cannot not alter where we've been, but in this moment, we can create a roadmap for our future.

We remember the past in the present, we think about the future in the present. **Today is the most important day we have.**

We cannot go to the past, but we can leverage our past experiences and make plans and set goals for our future. With the passage of time, we transform experiences into lessons. Lessons that help us shape our future.

Yes, we have the power to decide where we want to be, what we want to do, and with whom we want to be, in ten minutes - or ten years - from this moment.

There are many factors that can affect our plans, and our future may turn out a little - or a lot - different from what we envisioned. But if we know the direction, we will get to our destination sooner. Maybe we take a detour or a shortcut, but we will get there. Adjusting to circumstances is easier when we have an overall sense of where we are heading.

Goal setting is an easy task for some and a monumental task for others. My hope is that whatever your comfort level is with personal goal setting, this book can assist you in setting and defining your goals, identifying your priorities, and maximizing your efforts.

We will use the concept of a time capsule to document your goals and your life vision.

I decided to call the book Time Capsule 2030 because we are

embarking on a new decade and 2030 seems like an excellent point to use as a destination in time.

I wrote this book as a tool to do long-term personal planning. The ideas I am going to share can be applied to short and mid-term goal setting as well.

Consider this a guide. You are going to be doing all the work. My comments and the quotes I have included are to motivate and give a roadmap to set your life vision and goals.

You can decide if you want to spend few minutes a day working on your roadmap, or power through it over a weekend.

If reading this book makes you smile, reflect, act, or stop and think where you have been, where you are, and where you are going, I will be happy, and I will consider this book a success.

There are three sections:

In **Section One**, you will create your own definition of a time capsule and answer some questions about where you are and where you want to be. Your notes will reflect your overall plan and provide a glimpse of your life today to your 2030 self.

In **Section Two**, you will set two to five goals for several of the most important aspects of your life.

In **Section Three**, we will discuss the Life Dimensions Matrix™. This is a simple exercise but a telling one.

The book contains exercises for you to participate in, and empty pages for you to write your answers and notes. Feel free to use a separate notebook or computer, or photocopy these pages instead.

Personally, I always use a notebook, because it is amazing how detailed the answer to a simple question can be. Sometimes we just need a small prompt to open the gates to a sea of words.

Are you ready to start working on your time capsule? Let's go!

"The greatest masterpieces were once only pigments on a palette."

Henry S. Haskins

Setting the Tone
First Section

Monique McVeigh

Time Capsule

A time capsule is defined by the ***New Oxford American Dictionary*** as "a container storing a selection of objects chosen as being typical of the present time, buried for discovery in the future."

What if instead of making a traditional time capsule, we make a time capsule with our goals and notes on how we envision our lives will be in 2030? A life capsule, to be discovered by our older selves.

Let's work on personalizing your own time capsule.

Regarding the definition above, for your time capsule, your "container" is your notes in this book (or journal/diary). Your "selection of objects" to include is your thoughts, goals, hopes, wishes, and dreams.

For the dates of "present time" and "buried for discovery in the future," you can personalize it or leave it the same.

My personal definition is: *"My time capsule is the blue notebook with my life vision and goals as recorded in December 2019, buried to be discovered in 2030."*

I kept the word "buried," because I know myself. My 2030 time capsule will be buried after a few weeks under folders with drafts, correspondence, and books, or tucked away in the drawer where I keep all my socks.

If you want, you can go to the back yard and literally bury your time capsule. Personally, I'd forget where I placed it, and would dig in the wrong spot, repeatedly, until the yard looked like there was a gopher infestation.

I recommend not burying it until you finish reading Section 3.

What is your definition of your 2030 time capsule?

_____

_____

_____

_____

Time Capsule 2030

_____

_____

_____

_____

_____

_____

_____

_____

_____

_____

You may be wondering how creating your own definition of a time capsule will help you to define and document your goals. By creating a personalized definition, you became engaged in the process. You made your first decision, and have chosen what you are going to use to write or record your goals, objectives, and thoughts.

You've completed your first step in goal planning!

Are you ready to explore your 2030 vision?

"The journey of a thousand miles begins with one step."

Lao Tzu

Monique McVeigh

For you

When completing the exercises in this book, it is important to be 100% honest with yourself. This is for you. It is an opportunity to look inside, to express what your aspirations, goals, and desires are for the future. It is an opportunity to visualize how you want your life to be.

Think about where you want to be, what you want to be doing, and who you want to be associated with.

The goal of this book is to help guide you in setting a direction for your life, or to discover that you already have a direction you were unaware of.

By articulating your desires and thoughts, they are brought to the forefront, to a level of consciousness.

You may realize in the next pages that you need to make some life adjustments in order to reach your goals. Adjustments that are not necessarily easy or pleasant. You could find that you have avoided dealing with a person or situation, which has become a roadblock that impedes you from reaching your goals.

Unsolved issues can drain your energy, energy that can be utilized to reach your goals.

Please be sincere with yourself; this is a tool for you. On occasion, we need to change, and we often avoid change because it makes us uncomfortable. Change sometimes demands that we come out of our comfort zone, which is never easy. Maintaining the status quo is an option, but is it really what you want? Do you want to look back to this moment in 2030 and see that your life has not changed because you decided to stay within your comfort zone?

This book can become the catalyst to bring to the surface situations that have been percolating in the back of your mind and that need to be addressed for you to achieve your full potential.

You might want to share your goals with others. Why? Because for some, the only way to achieve them is with the help of others. Also, sharing a goal will make you feel more accountable for it. Making your intentions known to others helps make your goals more real.

Time Capsule 2030

You can share as much or as little about what you are going to write in this book. But you should not shortchange yourself by refusing to be 100% sincere.

Cheers to making your dreams reality!

Cheers to achieving your goals!

Cheers to finding where you want to be in 2030!

"Those who are outside their door already have a hard part of their journey behind them."

Dutch Proverb

Today

Imagine it's the morning of January 1st, 2030, and you're sitting in a comfortable place, listening to your favorite music or enjoying a peaceful moment.

In that moment, the first morning of 2030, **what do you want your older self to remember from today, from this period in your life?**

_____
_____
_____
_____
_____
_____
_____
_____
_____
_____
_____
_____
_____
_____
_____
_____

Time Capsule 2030

___

"There was a wise man in the East whose constant prayer was that he might see today with the eyes of tomorrow."

Alfred Mercier

Visualize

The following quote is one of my favorites:

"I saw the angel in the marble and carved until I set him free."

Michelangelo

There is no time machine to take us to the future to see how our lives turn out. The closest thing we have is visualization. We can make a clear picture of what we want our life to be in 2030 from the comfort of our home. Our mind is powerful and visualization is key. Most professional athletes utilize visualization as part of their preparation.

By visualizing yourself in a situation, you are also thinking of how you are going to get there, consciously or unconsciously.

There are two ways to approach this exercise:
1. You can create a mental progression of your life, visualizing key moments from today taking you all the way to 2030, every time getting you closer to 2030.
2. You can think where you want to be in 2030 and then work your way backwards, visualizing what needs to happen in order to be where you want to be in 2030. How do you want to feel, physically and mentally? Create this image in your mind and then write it down.

This is your life vision, your overall goal. Now you need to convert it into reality. You need to be the Michelangelo of your life.

The first time I read the Michelangelo quote, I realized I was not living my life to the fullest. I was not setting free my ideas and desires. We can visualize all we want, but if we do not act, those pieces of marble are not going to carve themselves.

Opportunities in our lives are pieces of marble. The relationships in our lives are also pieces of marble.

Do not leave those pieces uncarved. Not everything turns out to be a masterpiece, but we will never know until we work on them.

What is the vision of your life in 2030?

_____
_____
_____
_____
_____
_____
_____
_____
_____
_____
_____
_____
_____
_____
_____
_____

Monique McVeigh

Happiness

Through life we experience different degrees of happiness. Sometimes we search for happiness and sometimes happiness finds us.

What is going to make you happy or happier between today and 2030? Why?

_____
_____
_____
_____
_____
_____
_____
_____
_____
_____
_____
_____
_____
_____
_____
_____
_____
_____

Monique McVeigh

___

"Happiness is when what you think, what you say, and what you do are in harmony."

Mahatma Gandhi

Inventory

Make a list of the activities, skills, individuals, and environments that will help you achieve your goals, feel better, and contribute to you being the person you want to be in the future.

_____

_____

_____

_____

_____

_____

_____

_____

_____

_____

_____

_____

_____

_____

_____

_____

_____

_____

Now, list the people and habits that will NOT contribute to you achieving your goals.

_____

_____

_____

_____

_____

_____

_____

_____

_____

_____

_____

_____

_____

"A person can grow only as much as his horizon allows."

John Powell

You make your horizon. You need to lay the foundation that will help you achieve your goals. Block by block, you are laying the path to your life vision. Not having the right blocks in place will make your journey more difficult than it needs to be.

Going Deeper
Second Section

Time Capsule 2030

So far, you have set up an overall vision of what you expect your life to be in 2030. Now it is time to dig deeper and set individual goals to achieve your 2030 life vision. In the following pages, you will need to explore the different areas of your life and come up with at least two goals for each of them.

The areas include:
- Business/Career
- Charity/Gratitude
- Family/Friends/Romance
- Financial
- Fun/Recreation/Social
- Health/Well-being
- Personal Development
- Spirituality

You may decide that you have additional categories that you want to focus on, or you may want to split one of the above categories into two. Feel free to, just be aware that too many categories will make it difficult to focus on your goals and track your progress.

It's also important to guard against getting so absorbed in pursuing one goal, that your focus on it leads to neglecting other areas of your life.

In the following pages, you will be putting the spotlight on the different areas of your life.

Write two to five goals for each category. If you have more than five goals, go ahead and write them down, but only after you have written at least two goals for each of the categories.

When writing your goals, be sure to identify the timeframe when you will accomplish them. The dates do not need to be exact; the month, season, quarter or year will be fine. Remember: *you are setting goals to reach your 2030 vision. If your 2030 vision is a puzzle, the goals are the pieces.*

As an example, the following page includes three goals of my 2030 life vision.

From Monique's 2030 Life Vision
Business/Career Dimension

> 1) By 2022, have at least 4 books published in two languages.
>
> 2) In 2024, be a speaker at the Central Coast Writers Conference.
>
> 3) By 2027, have attended the major book fairs: Book Expo USA , The London Book Fair, Madrid, Frankfurter Buchmesse, and Feria Internacional del Libro.

I guess now that I have made public my goals, I will need to post updates in social media!

Now it's time to write your goals.

"A good goal is like a strenuous exercise – it makes you stretch."

Mary Kay Ash

Time Capsule 2030

Business/Career

Write two to five goals.

_____

_____

_____

_____

_____

_____

_____

_____

_____

_____

_____

_____

_____

_____

_____

_____

_____

_____

Monique McVeigh

"Choose a job you love, and you will never have to work a day in your life."

Confucius

Charity/Gratitude

Write two to five goals.

Monique McVeigh

"What you leave behind is not what is engraved in stone monuments, but what is woven into the lives of others."

Pericles

Family/Friends/Romance

Write two to five goals.

Monique McVeigh

"The bitterest tears shed over graves are for words left unsaid and deeds left undone."

Harriet Beecher Stowe

Time Capsule 2030

Financial

Write two to five goals.

Monique McVeigh

"If you would know the value of money, go and try to borrow some."

Benjamin Franklin

Fun/Recreation/Social

Write two to five goals.

Monique McVeigh

"Zest is the secret of all beauty. There is no beauty that is attractive without zest."

Christian Dior

Health/Well-being

Write two to five goals.

Monique McVeigh

"To love oneself is the beginning of a lifelong romance."

Oscar Wilde

Time Capsule 2030

Personal Development

Write two to five goals.

Monique McVeigh

"Educate yourself beyond a degree. Learn to question; to develop your own thoughts, and how to structure an effective logical argument; learn to give and to love."

D. Paul Graham

Spiritual

Write two to five goals.

Monique McVeigh

"Invest in the human soul who knows, it might be a diamond in the rough."

Mary McLeod Bethune

One more goal

Write at least one goal related to ADVENTURE.

This goal should be the one that will take you out of your comfort zone. Is there something in your life that you've always wanted to do, but end up putting aside?

For example, I've always wanted to take a tango lesson, but have made multiple arguments and excuses not to do it: I need to find a partner, I do not want to take a group class (no need for witnesses), the classes are too far away, and the list keeps going. Are any of those reasons insurmountable? Not at all. The main reason I haven't signed up is, while I love to dance and I do not have any issue being the first one on the dance floor dancing alone, everything changes when it requires holding someone else. I become clumsy and I step on my partner's feet. Even slow, romantic songs are difficult for me.

One of my goals is to take tango lessons before 2021. Who knows, I may enjoy them enough to take group lessons, or want to learn different styles. But I will never know if I do not take the first step and sign up for the first lesson.

"If you are never scared or embarrassed or hurt, it means you never take any chances."

Julia Sorel

Adventure

Write at least one goal.

_____
_____
_____
_____
_____
_____
_____
_____
_____
_____
_____
_____
_____
_____
_____
_____

"Once we accept our limits, we go beyond them."

Albert Einstein

Life Dimensions Matrix™
Third Section

Time and Energy

Time is a limited resource, and our energy also has limitations. How often do we find ourselves with a list of things to do in a day, only to realize by noon that we haven't made a dent in it?

Sometimes we want to do more than what is possible. In those moments, the best way to spend our time is not tackling the first item on the list, but prioritizing what should be first on the list.

Prioritization is imperative in order to achieve goals and to make the best use of time and energy.

There are two reasons why you were asked to provide two to five goals for each category:

First, we have the tendency to favor one aspect of our life, but by doing so, we do not always pay attention to the others. For example, if somebody's highest priority is to get the next promotion and climb the corporate ladder, her/his goals may be focused exclusively around the Business/Career dimension. The other dimensions may be overlooked, and can suffer. Months can pass, years even, before the person discovers that the other areas in her/his life were ignored for too long. Or it can also work the other way: we pay attention to most areas of our lives but there is one that we neglect. Whether intentional or not, we postpone addressing it, over and over, and sometimes never giving it the focus it deserves.

Second, with limited time and energy, we need to maximize our efforts.

The next steps will involve writing on the Life Dimensions Matrix™, on pages 49, 51, 53 and 55. As before, feel free to cut these pages out or photocopy them.

For the first step, go back to page 20 and number each goal. Next, take the matrix sheet and put the number of the goal and a keyword to help you identify the goal under the boxes assigned in the first column of the matrix. Repeat this step for each category.

The second step is, for each goal, put a check mark under the other dimensions if the goal has an impact on, is affected by, or is related to the other areas in your life (life dimensions).

For the final step, use the circles to the left of each life dimension to rank your current level of happiness/satisfaction with each area in your life. Use a scale of 1 to 10, 1 being the least satisfied and 10 completely satisfied. Also, put an "A" next to the goal that will push you beyond your comfort level and could qualify as an Adventure goal.

Page 43 has two examples of my personal Life Dimensions Matrix™.

As an example, in 2018 I set a goal to organize a trip with my brother and his family. 2017 had been a difficult time for him. Early in the year, he became sick, and the reason was not immediately clear. After several months, the doctors discovered he had two health conditions, which he will need to deal with for the rest of his life. Once he was doing better, I thought he and his family could celebrate with a relaxing trip to a beautiful tropical beach.

This was a goal under my Family dimension/category. But it was also related to the Gratitude, Financial, Fun, Well-being, and Personal Development categories. Gratitude, because I was happy my brother was doing better, and we could celebrate. Financial, because I had to save for the trip. Recreational, because well, having a vacation is always fun. Well-being too, as taking time from work is always great for recharging.

For me, this goal included a Personal Development component. I like to snorkel, but was not too comfortable in the water. In preparation for the trip, I took swimming lessons. The lessons were out of my comfort zone and the plan was to snorkel without a guide babysitting me all the time (which falls under the Adventure category as well).

The other goal included in the example is from my Personal Development category. After seeing a watercolor artist post a 60-second video making a geometrical watercolor drawing, I decided this was something I wanted to learn. I bought paper, brushes and pigments, and the book Everyday Watercolor, by Jenna Rainey. While it started as a Personal Development goal, I soon discovered that it was also having an impact on my Recreation and Well-being life dimensions.

Sometimes we do not realize the broad impact that our actions can have.

I am sure you will have at least one goal that is affected by or impacts several categories. We do not need to focus on too many goals, just the ones that will get us the most from our efforts. There are occasions where it is important to focus on one goal that is exclusive to one of the categories, because it may be imperative for our life vision to achieve it.

With limited time and energy, we need to prioritize what is important to start working on now vs. next month or next year. We cannot start working on everything at once, otherwise we can be overwhelmed. Remember: you are creating a long-term plan.

"Be aware of dissipating your powers; strive constantly to concentrate them."

Johann von Goethe

Dimension & Goals	Business/ Career	Charity/ Gratitude	Family/ Friends/ Romance	Financial	Fun/ Recreation/ Social	Health/ Well-being	Personal Development	Spirituality
Family/Friends/ Romance								
Take brother and his family on a trip		x		x	x	x		
Personal Development								
Watercolor Painting					x	x		

⑧ A

⑧

Monique McVeigh

Action Plan

Now that you have listed your goals and discovered that some are interrelated, you can select the ones you want (or need) to tackle first.

For the next step, set the dates for when you want to accomplish the goals you've selected.

With some of the larger goals, you may want to break them into smaller tasks. Going back to my family vacation example, my list of tasks included: determining travel dates based on spring break and hurricane season, pricing out hotels and flights, scheduling swimming lessons and making reservations for hotels, flights, and tours. Each of these had a timeline.

Do this for the goals that are short-term and the goals that that will require you to start taking steps today, even if they won't be accomplished for a few years.

When I decided to pursue a graduate degree, my goal was to graduate in four years. It was going to take one year to prep for the GMAT exam and complete the application process for the two schools to which I applied. Then, after being admitted, I had three years of evening classes while working full-time.

"Nothing is particularly hard if we divide it into small jobs."

Henry Ford

Time Capsule 2030

Revisiting, Reviewing, and Updating

The next step is to determine when you want to do a check-in, and go over your goals.

Schedule two or three meetings during the year with yourself. No distractions, just you and your 2030 life vision, your goals, and your Life Dimensions Matrix™.

I usually revisit my goals at the beginning of spring, sometime in summer, and at the end of the year. If something major has occurred in my life, I may look to see how it affects the plans that I have laid out.

You will need to come back and look at the goals that were put on the back burner and decide if they should still be on the list, or if they have become irrelevant for achieving your vision for 2030. Some may stay, and others may be replaced with new goals. Your plan will be adapted to where you are at that moment in your life. The only constant in our lives is change.

Your overall vision for 2030 is likely to change, too. At the very least, you may need to make some adjustments along the way to get there. You may have found a shortcut or need to take a detour to get to your destination. Or you may decide that you need a totally new destination.

Also, when you are reviewing your Life Dimensions Matrix™, ask yourself how happy or satisfied you are with each life dimension. Be sincere with yourself. If there is something that needs to be addressed, this is the time to do it.

Remember that I mentioned that you may not want to bury this book as an actual time capsule, as you will need to refer to it from time to time to see how you are doing.

If you still want to bury a time capsule, you can cut pages 10, 11, 13 and 15. Or you can make a copy of them.

I wish you the best in your future!

About Monique McVeigh

Monique McVeigh is a successful financial executive with over twenty years of experience in business management, financial planning and accounting. She has been instrumental in ensuring business units operate efficiently and comply with best practices while achieving their financial and tactical objectives.

She earned an MBA from the University of Southern California with concentrations in Corporate Finance and Marketing.

In her spare time, she enjoys hiking, reading, writing poetry in Spanish and practicing restorative yoga.

She lives in the Southwest of the United States with her two Siamese cats.

Connect with Monique McVeigh online:
Facebook.com/Monique.McVeigh.Author
Instagram: @MoniqueMcVeighAuthor

Monique McVeigh

Templates

Dimension & Goals	Business/ Career	Charity/ Gratitude	Family/ Friends/ Romance	Financial	Fun/ Recreation/ Social	Health/ Well-being	Personal Development	Spirituality
Business/ Career								
Charity/Gratitude								

Dimension & Goals	Business/ Career	Charity/ Gratitude	Family/ Friends/ Romance	Financial	Fun/ Recreation/ Social	Health/ Well-being	Personal Development	Spirituality
Family/Friends/ Romance								
Financial								

Dimension & Goals	Busi- ness/ Career	Charity/ Gratitude	Family/ Friends/ Romance	Financial	Fun/ Recreation/ Social	Health/ Well-being	Personal Development	Spirituality
Fun/Recreation/ Social								
Health/Well-being								

Dimension & Goals	Business/ Career	Charity/ Gratitude	Family/ Friends/ Romance	Financial	Fun/ Recreation/ Social	Health/ Well-being	Personal Development	Spirituality
Personal Development								
Spirituality								

www.ingramcontent.com/pod-product-compliance
Lightning Source LLC
Chambersburg PA
CBHW070049230426
43661CB00005B/833